Beautiful Mandalas
Coloring Book For Adults

Celoris™

Copyright © 2020 By Celoris

All rights reserved. No part of this publication may be reproduced, distributed, or transmitted in any form or by any means, including photocopying, recording, or other electronic or mechanical methods.